NIST Interagency Report 7692

Specification for the Open Checklist Interactive Language (OCIL) Version 2.0

David Waltermire
Karen Scarfone
Maria Casipe

COMPUTER SECURITY

Computer Security Division
Information Technology Laboratory
National Institute of Standards and Technology
Gaithersburg, MD 20899-8930

April 2011

U.S. Department of Commerce

Gary Locke, Secretary

National Institute of Standards and Technology

Dr. Patrick D. Gallagher, Director

Reports on Computer Systems Technology

The Information Technology Laboratory (ITL) at the National Institute of Standards and Technology (NIST) promotes the U.S. economy and public welfare by providing technical leadership for the nation's measurement and standards infrastructure. ITL develops tests, test methods, reference data, proof of concept implementations, and technical analysis to advance the development and productive use of information technology. ITL's responsibilities include the development of technical, physical, administrative, and management standards and guidelines for the cost-effective security and privacy of sensitive unclassified information in Federal computer systems. This Interagency Report discusses ITL's research, guidance, and outreach efforts in computer security and its collaborative activities with industry, government, and academic organizations.

Acknowledgments

The authors, David Waltermire of NIST, Karen Scarfone of G2, Inc., and Maria Casipe of the MITRE Corporation, wish to thank their colleagues who reviewed drafts of this report and contributed to its technical content. The authors would like to acknowledge Paul Cichonski and Stephen Quinn of NIST; Charles Schmidt, Andrew Buttner, Jon Baker, Gerry McGuire, and John Wunder of the MITRE Corporation; Rhonda Farrell of Booz Allen Hamilton; and Glenn Strickland and George Saylor of G2, Inc. for their insights and support throughout the development of the report.

Abstract

This report defines version 2.0 of the Open Checklist Interactive Language (OCIL). The intent of OCIL is to provide a standardized basis for expressing questionnaires and related information, such as answers to questions and final questionnaire results, so that the questionnaires can use a standardized, machine-readable approach to interacting with humans and using information stored during previous data collection efforts. OCIL documents are Extensible Markup Language (XML) based. This report defines and explains the requirements that IT products and OCIL documents asserting conformance with the OCIL 2.0 specification must meet.

Audience

The primary audiences for the OCIL specification are developers of IT products that could leverage OCIL's capabilities and organizations that could take advantage of OCIL to improve questionnaire-based data gathering from people and from previous data collection efforts. NIST welcomes feedback from these groups on improving the OCIL specification.

Table of Contents

List of Figures and Tables

1. Introduction

The Open Checklist Interactive Language (OCIL) defines a framework for expressing questionnaires that can be used by software to harvest information stored during previous data collection efforts or to collect information from people. OCIL allows organizations to author questionnaires in a standardized format that can be processed by a variety of software products. OCIL also includes constructs for representing such things as questions, instructions that guide users towards an answer, and submission of user-provided documents that provide evidence for responses.

OCIL facilitates uniform data collection and reporting. Other benefits of using OCIL include:
- Performing every manual check in the same manner with all required steps followed, regardless of who performs the check.
- Allowing responses to manual checks to be reviewed for auditing purposes.
- Fostering the development of standardized, interoperable capabilities in products for creating, evaluating, and supporting manual checks.
- Fostering collaboration among security-related communities in authoring and composing manual checks.
- Enhancing the manageability of manual checks.

The original motivation for creating OCIL was for development of automated security checklist questionnaires for human interaction. OCIL can be used to help assess security controls related to people and processes when assessment is not feasible or possible with fully automated means. An example is asking users about their participation in security training as part of an automated approach to Federal Information Security Management Act (FISMA) compliance reporting or to support a standardized means for presenting information and evaluating users as part of a security awareness and training program. However, OCIL's capabilities can be applied to collect human input on any topic. For instance, it can be used for authoring research surveys and academic course exams. OCIL can also be used to harvest information stored during previous data collection efforts and convert it to a standardized format, which can then more easily be aggregated with other data sources and accessed through a single interface, such as a dashboard. Many of the examples presented in this document are security-related, but this is not intended to imply any limitation on OCIL's applicability.

1.1 Purpose and Scope

The purpose of this report is to define version 2.0 of OCIL. This report defines and explains the requirements that producers of OCIL-supporting software and OCIL documents (questionnaires) must meet to claim conformance with the OCIL 2.0 specification.

This report only applies to version 2.0 of OCIL. All other versions are out of the scope of this report.

1.2 Document Structure

The remainder of this document is organized into the following major sections and appendices:
- Section 2 defines terms used within this specification and provides a list of common acronyms and other abbreviations.
- Section 3 defines the conformance rules for this specification.
- Section 4 provides an overview of related specifications and standards.
- Section 5 presents the primary components of the OCIL data model.

- Section 6 provides requirements and recommendations for OCIL content syntax, structures, and development.
- Section 7 describes OCIL document processing requirements.
- Appendix A discusses possible use cases for OCIL.
- Appendix B defines requirements for using OCIL as a check system for the eXtensible Configuration Checklist Description Format (XCCDF).

1.3 Document Conventions

The key words "MUST", "MUST NOT", "REQUIRED", "SHALL", "SHALL NOT", "SHOULD", "SHOULD NOT", "RECOMMENDED", "MAY", and "OPTIONAL" in this document are to be interpreted as described in *Request for Comment (RFC) 2119.* [1]

Text intended to represent computing system input, output, or algorithmic processing is presented in `fixed-width Courier font`.

1.4 Feedback

OCIL currently does not address:
- A specific method for identifying the subject or role to present an OCIL-based assessment to. This might be addressed by another specification in the future.
- Specific guidelines on how to report on the evaluation of OCIL questionnaires relating to a population of IT assets
- A reference architecture for integrating OCIL with other XCCDF check systems to perform a more complete assessment of a checklist
- Specific guidelines on using questionnaires to collect answers strictly for informational purposes, instead of for compliance purposes. Although OCIL has no requirements that it be used for compliance purposes only, its statuses and results are oriented toward compliance goals, and informational use cases are not explicitly addressed in this specification.
- A method for applying a digital signature to OCIL results. Because the current OCIL data model does not address this, it is assumed that digital signatures should be handled external to the OCIL data model.

The development of OCIL as a language strongly depends on community response, suggestions, and feedback. Feedback in these and any other areas is needed in order to improve OCIL in future revisions of this report. Thus, the authors welcome your comments about the OCIL specification. They can be reached at ocil-comments@nist.gov.

---

[1] RFC 2119, "Key words for use in RFCs to Indicate Requirement Levels", is available at http://www.ietf.org/rfc/rfc2119.txt.

2.   Definitions and Acronyms

This section defines selected terms and acronyms used within the document.

2.1   Definitions

The definitions below are for the basic elements of OCIL content. Other terms are defined throughout the rest of the publication.

artifact: A piece of evidence, such as text or a reference to a resource, that is submitted to support a response to a question.

question: The text of a question to pose, optionally accompanied by instructions to help guide a person to a response.

questionnaire: A sequence of questions to be used in determining a state or condition.

results: All data acquired from using a questionnaire, such as the answers to individual questions and the final result for the entire questionnaire.

test action: The action to be performed based on the response to a particular question. Examples of test actions are asking another question or calculating a result.

variable: A logical entity that holds a single value.

2.2   Acronyms

API	Application Programming Interface
CCE	Common Configuration Enumeration
CPE	Common Platform Enumeration
CSRC	Computer Security Resource Center
CVE	Common Vulnerabilities and Exposures
FISMA	Federal Information Security Management Act
IR	Interagency Report
IT	Information Technology
ITL	Information Technology Laboratory
MIME	Multipurpose Internet Mail Extensions
NIST	National Institute of Standards and Technology
OCIL	Open Checklist Interactive Language
OMB	Office of Management and Budget
OVAL	Open Vulnerability and Assessment Language
PCI-DSS	Payment Card Industry Data Security Standard
RFC	Request for Comment
SP	Special Publication
URL	Uniform Resource Locator
XCCDF	eXtensible Configuration Checklist Description Format
XML	eXtensible Markup Language

3. Conformance

Products and organizations may want to claim conformance with this specification for a variety of reasons. For example, a software vendor may want to assert that its product uses OCIL content properly and can interoperate with any other product using proper OCIL content. Another example is a policy mandating that an organization use OCIL for documenting and executing security audit questionnaires, as well as storing their results.

This section provides the high-level requirements that a product or OCIL document must meet for conformance with this specification. Most of the requirements listed in this section reference other sections in the document that fully define the requirements.

Other specifications that use OCIL may define additional requirements and recommendations for OCIL's use. Such requirements and recommendations are outside the scope of this publication.

3.1 Product Conformance

All products claiming conformance with this specification SHALL adhere to the following requirements:

1. Products that process OCIL documents SHALL consume and correctly process well-formed OCIL documents. This includes following all of the processes defined in Section 7.

2. Products that produce OCIL documents SHALL ensure that all OCIL documents they produce are well-formed. This includes following all of the processes defined in Section 7, and adhering to the syntax, structural, and other OCIL document development requirements defined in Section 6.

3. If the product uses OCIL as a check system for XCCDF (as described in Appendix A), then the product SHALL adhere to the requirements defined in Appendix B.

4. Make an explicit claim of conformance to this specification in any documentation provided to end users.

3.2 Organization Conformance

Organizations creating or maintaining OCIL documents that claim conformance with this specification SHALL follow these requirements:

1. Adhere to the official OCIL schema as explained in Section 5.

2. Adhere to the syntax, structural, and other OCIL document development requirements defined in Section 6.

3. For OCIL documents to be used in a check system for XCCDF (as described in Appendix A), adhere to the requirements defined in Appendix B.

4. Relationships to Existing Specifications and Standards

This section is primarily informative, and is intended to define the relationships between this specification and any other related specifications or standards (both current and past).[2]

4.1 Relationship to OVAL

The Open Vulnerability and Assessment Language (OVAL) is used to express standardized, machine-readable rules that can be used to assess the state of a system. In the domain of information security, OVAL is commonly used to determine the presence of vulnerabilities and insecure software configurations through automated means. OVAL reports its findings in a standardized XML-based manner.

OVAL and OCIL complement each other and they can be considered peers. OVAL is used to collect specified pieces of information from systems directly and automatically, without human interaction; OCIL is used to collect specified pieces of information by harvesting existing sources of collected data or by asking a human to supply it. Both OVAL and OCIL produce XML-based reports, which supports aggregation of OVAL and OCIL results.

4.2 Relationship to XCCDF

Extensible Configuration Checklist Description Format (XCCDF) is a specification language for expressing security configuration checklists and other sets of system assessment rules. XCCDF provides a standardized means of expressing these sets of rules and the results of evaluating a system using these rules.

XCCDF rules do not directly specify how checks should be performed; instead, these rules point to other XML documents, such as OVAL definition files and OCIL document files, which contain the actual instructions for performing the checks. Appendix A describes a use case involving using OCIL as a check system for XCCDF, and Appendix B provides syntax, processing, and other requirements for such a use case.

---

[2]   Most of the information in this section is derived from NIST SP 800-126 Revision 1, *The Technical Specification for the Security Content Automation Protocol (SCAP): SCAP Version 1.1* (http://csrc.nist.gov/publications/PubsSPs.html).

5.   Data Model Overview

This section provides an overview of the data model that all OCIL implementations MUST support. It describes the data that is required to support common OCIL use cases. This section uses the term "element" to identify the classes within the data model, and the term "property" to identify any properties of a class. This section only defines selected aspects of the data model. The XML schema implementation of this model, which is the authoritative XML binding definition, can be found at http://scap.nist.gov/schema/ocil/2.0/ocil-2.0.xsd.

5.1   The ocil Element

An ocil element contains all questionnaires, test_actions, questions, artifacts, variables, and results for an OCIL document, as well as document metadata. The table below describes the ocil element's properties.

ocil

Property	Type	Count	Description
generator (element)	GeneratorType	1	Information related to the generation of the document, including the OCIL schema version, the time of the document's generation, the name and version of the application used to generate it, and the name(s) of the document's author(s).
document (element)	DocumentType	0-1	Document-level information that MAY be presented to a user, including title, descriptions, and notices.
questionnaires (element)	QuestionnairesType	1	A container for all questionnaire elements. Each questionnaire describes a sequence of questions that MAY be posed to determine a state or condition, including processing instructions.
test_actions (element)	TestActionsType	1	A container for all test_action elements. Each test_action describes a state or condition that MAY be checked for, including processing instructions.
questions (element)	QuestionsType	1	A container for all types of question and choice_group elements. - Each question describes what SHALL be posed when checking for a particular state or condition. - Each choice_group represents a reusable set of choices for a choice_question. A choice_question MAY reference a choice_group or explicitly specify allowed choices.
artifacts (element)	ArtifactsType	0-1	A container for all artifact elements, which define the types of artifacts to be collected. An artifact MAY be retrieved during evaluation, as evidence to support a response to a question.
variables (element)	VariablesType	0-1	A container for all types of variables (e.g., constant, local, and external) elements. Each variable SHALL hold a single value computed based on its source.

Property	Type	Count	Description
results (element)	ResultsType	0-1	Assessment data generated during the evaluation of questionnaires, test_actions, and questions; includes the collection of artifacts and artifact metadata, if applicable.

The rest of Section 5 provides additional information on each of these properties.

5.2 The generator Element

The generator element contains information about the generation of the OCIL document file. The properties of the generator element are listed below. Organizations MAY supply additional information not covered by these properties, but such information is not part of the official OCIL language.

generator

Property	Type	Count	Description
product_name (element)	normalizedString	0-1	The name of the application used to generate the file.
product_version (element)	normalizedString	0-1	The version of the application used to generate the file.
author (element)	UserType	0-n	Authors of the document.
schema_version (element)	decimal	1	The version of the OCIL schema that the document was written in and that should be used for validation.
timestamp (element)	dateTime	1	When the OCIL document was generated.
additional_data (element)	ExtensionContainerType	0-1	A container for metadata extensions about the generator used to create the OCIL document.

5.3 The document Element

The document element holds document-level information such as the title. The properties of the document element are listed below.

document

Property	Type	Count	Description
title (element)	normalizedString	1	The title of the document.
description (element)	normalizedString	0-n	An overall description for the entire document.
notice (element)	string	0-n	A notice or warning to the user of the document.

5.4 The questionnaire Element

The questionnaire element is the basic unit of an OCIL check. It contains references to sequences of questions and test_actions that are used to determine a state or condition. The properties of a questionnaire element are described below.

questionnaire

Property	Type	Count	Description
id (attribute)	QuestionnaireIDPattern	1	Unique identifier for a questionnaire element.
child_only (attribute)	boolean	0-1	Whether the questionnaire SHALL be treated as a child-level questionnaire only (=true) or can be treated as both a child-level and top-level questionnaire (=false). (By default: false.) A child-level questionnaire can only be referenced by test_action elements, and not called directly as a top-level questionnaire.
title (element)	TextType	0-1	Heading or caption that describes the questionnaire.
description (element)	TextType	0-1	Text that describes the questionnaire in more detail than a title.
references (element)	ReferencesType	0-1	Information about any external references related to this questionnaire. Examples MAY include references to other standards, including but not limited to CVE, CCE, or CPE.
actions (element)	OperationType	1	A container for one or more test_action_ref elements, along with the methods used to combine their results into a single result.
notes (element)	string	0-n	Any additional information related to the questionnaire.

The following table defines the properties of the actions element mentioned in the previous table.

actions

Property	Type	Count	Description
test_action_ref (element)	TestActionRefType	1-n	Identifiers of one or more test_action elements.
operation (attribute)	OperatorType	0-1	How to aggregate (AND, OR) the results of a set of test_actions. (By default: AND.)
negate (attribute)	boolean	0-1	Whether the result should be toggled from PASS to FAIL and vice versa. Any result other than PASS or FAIL will be unchanged by a negate operation. (By default: false.)

8

5.5   The test_action Element

A test_action is used to identify a specific question to pose, and then handle the response. Handling the response can involve picking a specific result value for this test_action, as listed in Section 7.2, or calling another test_action or questionnaire. The test_action element itself is abstract and SHALL NOT appear within an OCIL document. It is extended by the question_test_action element. The properties of the question_test_action element are listed below.

question_test_action

Property	Type	Count	Description
id (attribute)	QuestionTestActionIDPattern	1	Unique identifier for a question_test_action.
question_ref (attribute)	QuestionIDPattern	1	Identifies a question using its id.
title (element)	TextType	0-1	Descriptive heading or caption that describes the question_test action.
when_unknown (element)	TestActionConditionType	0-1	Action to perform when an UNKNOWN value is received.
when_not_tested (element)	TestActionConditionType	0-1	Action to perform when a NOT_TESTED value is received.
when_not_applicable (element)	TestActionConditionType	0-1	Action to perform when a NOT_APPLICABLE value is received.
when_error (element)	TestActionConditionType	0-1	Action to perform when an ERROR value is received.
notes (element)	string	0-n	Additional information related to the test_action.

The question_test_action is extended by four different child elements, each of which corresponds to a different data type for the user response. It is these latter elements that SHALL be used in an OCIL document; the question_test_action element is abstract and SHALL NOT appear within an OCIL document. The child elements inherit all the properties of their parents, and each also defines additional properties related to the user response data type. Listed below are the additional properties of these four child elements: boolean_question_test_action, choice_question_test_action, numeric_question_test_action, and string_question_test_action.

A boolean_question_test_action is used for questions answered by YES/NO or TRUE/FALSE.

boolean_question_test_action

Property	Type	Count	Description
when_true (element)	TestActionConditionType	1	Action to perform when the response is TRUE or YES.
when_false (element)	TestActionConditionType	1	Action to perform when the response is FALSE or NO.

A choice_question_test_action is used when the user is presented with a list of possible responses and selects a single answer from the list.

Note: Choosing multiple answers is not supported by the data model at this time. If responding to multiple answers is desired then additional choices should be provided that combine multiple answers. For example, if choice A, B and C are offered, additional choices might be defined for A and B, B and C or "all of the above".

choice_question_test_action

Property	Type	Count	Description
when_choice (element)	ChoiceTestAction ConditionType	1-n	Action to perform when the response is one of a specified list of choices.

A numeric_question_test_action is used for questions answered with a numeric value.

numeric_question_test_action

Property	Type	Count	Description
when_equals (element)	EqualsTestAction ConditionType	0-n	Action to perform when the response is a specific numeric value.
when_range (element)	RangeTestAction ConditionType	0-n	Action to perform when the response falls within a specified range of values.

Although either when_equals or when_range MAY be omitted, at least one instance of one of them must appear within the body of a numeric_question_test_action. If multiple handlers could potentially match a particular response (for example, if there were overlapping ranges) then the first matching handler is used based on the order they appear within the document. Since when_equals handlers always come before when_range handlers, this gives when_equals handlers precedence.

A string_question_test_action is used for questions answered with a string.

string_question_test_action

Property	Type	Count	Description
when_pattern (element)	PatternTestAction ConditionType	1-n	Action to perform when the response is a string that matches a specified regular expression. If the response could match multiple patterns, the handler with the first matching pattern is used.

All four types of child elements (boolean_question_test_action, choice_question_test_action, numeric_question_test_action, and string_question_test_action) use elements of the TestActionConditionType. The properties of a TestActionConditionType are as follows:

TestActionConditionType

Property	Type	Count	Description
result (element)	ResultType	1, either result or test_action_ref but not both (XOR)	A final value (e.g., PASS, FAIL, ERROR, UNKNOWN, NOT_TESTED, NOT_APPLICABLE) to be returned. See Section 7.2 for additional information on result types.

10

Property	Type	Count	Description
test_action_ref (element)	TestActionRefType		Reference to a new test_action or questionnaire to be processed.
artifact_refs (element)	ArtifactRefsType	0-1	References to all the types of artifacts to be requested during evaluation. Contains a collection of one or more artifact_ref elements.

An artifact_ref element defines a single reference to a type of artifact (the basic information indicating which artifact is to be collected during processing).

artifact_ref

Property	Type	Count	Description
idref (attribute)	ArtifactIDPattern	1	Unique identifier for a type of artifact.
required (attribute)	boolean	0-1	Specifies whether the artifact must be included or not during processing. If true, then the questionnaire is not considered complete without the artifact; otherwise the artifact is desired but not necessary. The default value is false.

5.6 The questions Element

A questions element contains all of the questions and supporting information defined within the document.

questions

Property	Type	Count	Description
question (element)	QuestionType	1-n	Information for questions to be answered.
choice_group (element)	ChoiceGroupType	0-n	Holds groups that represent possible sets of choices for choice_questions.

A question element represents a question with REQUIRED text to pose and an OPTIONAL set of instructions for the user to follow to arrive at his or her answer.

question

Property	Type	Count	Description
id (attribute)	QuestionIDPattern	1	Unique identifier for a question.
question_text (element)	QuestionTextType	1-n	Provides the text of the question to be posed. The text MAY contain one or more values provided through variables.
instructions (element)	InstructionsType	0-1	A sequence of steps intended to guide the user in determining an answer to a question.

11

Property	Type	Count	Description
notes (element)	string	0-n	Any additional information related to the question.

The question element itself is abstract and SHALL NOT appear in OCIL documents. Instead, the four child elements—boolean_question, choice_question, numeric_question, and string_question, one for each data type of response—SHALL be used. Each is designed to handle a particular type of data for a valid answer. The child elements all inherit the constructs of their parent element. Additional properties of the child elements are shown below.

boolean_question

Property	Type	Count	Description
default_answer (attribute)	boolean	0-1	The default value of the question.
model (attribute)	BooleanQuestionModelType	0-1	Whether the response should be in the set {TRUE, FALSE} or the set {YES, NO}. (Default: response can either be YES or NO.)

choice_question

Property	Type	Count	Description
choice (element)	ChoiceType	1-n (see note below table)	Information associated with the possible responses to this choice_question.
choice_group_ref (element)	ChoiceGroupIDPattern		A reference to a choice_group; the choices described in the choice_group are possible responses for this choice_question.
default_answer_ref (attribute)	ChoiceIDPattern	0-1	The choice ID of the default answer to this question.

The choice and choice_group_ref elements listed above MAY be interleaved and products SHALL present each choice or choice_group_ref in the order in which they appear in the OCIL document.

numeric_question

Property	Type	Count	Description
default_answer (attribute)	decimal	0-1	The default value of the question.

string_question

Property	Type	Count	Description
default_answer (attribute)	string	0-1	The default value of the question.

Figure 1 shows the basic relationships between questionnaires, test actions, and questions in a pseudocode-like manner. The figure is not intended to exhaustively define or describe any of the elements; rather, the focus is on how these elements reference each other. The first box, representing questionnaire 4, calls test action 6. Test action 6 then calls question 1. If the answer to question 1 is "true", then a result of "FAIL" is returned, otherwise test action 2 is called. Test action 2 calls question 4, which is a choice question. Based on which choice is selected as the answer, test action 2 returns a result of "FAIL" or "PASS".

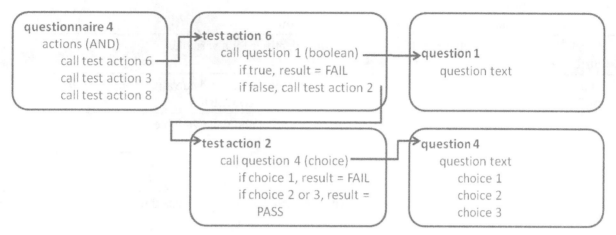

Figure 1. Relationships between Questionnaires, Test Actions, and Questions

5.7 The artifact element

An artifact element defines structures that contain information about an artifact, which is an object that serves as evidence for a question's answer. For example, if the question asks if a user has a defined process for maintaining system accounts, the artifact element would contain information about the type of process documentation that may need to be collected.

artifact

Property	Type	Count	Description
title (element)	TextType	1	A short summary or a caption about the artifact.
description (element)	TextType	1	Descriptive text about the artifact.
id (attribute)	ArtifactIDPattern	1	Unique identifier for an artifact.
persistent (attribute)	boolean	0-1	Specifies whether the artifact's existence is time sensitive or not. If the value is true, then a snapshot or a copy SHALL be kept. Otherwise, a pointer to the location of the artifact is enough. The default value is true.

5.8 The variable element

A variable is an abstract element that holds a single value computed based on its source. There are three derived classes: constant_variable, external_variable, and local_variable. These three classes SHALL be used in OCIL documents; the variable element, which is abstract, SHALL NOT be used.

The text of a question, which is held in the question_text element, MAY be customized by substituting values from one or more variables into the text.

13

The value for a constant_variable is defined by the author of the document.

constant_variable

Property	Type	Count	Description
id (attribute)	VariableIDPattern	1	Unique identifier for a variable.
datatype (attribute)	VariableDataType	1	Specifies how a variable data value should be treated or used (TEXT or NUMERIC).
description (element)	TextType	0-1	Descriptive text about the variable.
value (element)	string	1	A single variable data.
notes (element)	string	0-n	Any additional information related to the question.

The value of an external_variable is defined elsewhere, from an external source.

external_variable

Property	Type	Count	Description
id (attribute)	VariableIDPattern	1	Unique identifier for a variable.
datatype (attribute)	VariableDataType	1	Specifies how a variable data value should be treated or used (TEXT or NUMERIC).
description (element)	TextType	0-1	Descriptive text about the variable.
notes (element)	string	0-n	Any additional information related to the question.

The value of a local_variable is determined based on the answer to the question it links to (which is specified by the variable's question_ref element). This would be used to dynamically set the variable's value based on the answer to a previously asked question. If the local_variable has one or more set elements defined, the variable's value is computed based on those set elements, otherwise the variable's value is the same as the answer, with a few exceptions:

1. If the question is a boolean question and the variable data type is NUMERIC, then the value based on the answer is 1 for true and 0 for false.
2. If the question is a boolean question and the variable data type is TEXT, then the value is determined by the question's model as follows:
   a. MODEL_YES_NO: the value is "yes" if true or "no" if false.
   b. MODEL_TRUE_FALSE: the value is "true" if true or "false" if false.
3. If the question is a choice question, the variable data type is TEXT and the value is set to the text value of the choice.
4. If the question is a numeric question, the variable data type is NUMERIC then the value is set to the value of the answer.
5. If the question is a string question, the variable data type is TEXT then the value is set to the value of the answer.

The answer value is matched with patterns, choice_refs, ranges of values, and boolean values. Based on the match, the value of the local variable is set as defined.

local_variable

Property	Type	Count	Description
id (attribute)	VariableIDPattern	1	Unique identifier for a variable.
datatype (attribute)	VariableDataType	1	Specifies how a variable data value should be treated or used (TEXT or NUMERIC).
description (element)	TextType	0-1	Descriptive text about the variable.
question_ref (attribute)	QuestionIDPattern	1	Unique identifier of the question in which the variable is linked.
set (element)	VariableSetType	0-n	Information describing how to compute the value to be stored on the variable. Holds the pattern, choice_ref, range, or boolean values to be matched with the answer to the linked question, and the appropriate value to be stored on the variable based on the match.
notes (element)	string	0-n	Any additional information related to the question.

The set type and permitted datatype SHALL match the type of the question. The valid mappings are shown below:

Question Type	Set Type	Permitted Datatypes
boolean_question	when_boolean	NUMERIC (for 0, 1 answers) TEXT (for true, false answers and yes, no answers)
choice_question	when_choice	TEXT
numeric_question	when_range	NUMERIC
string_question	when_pattern	TEXT

5.9   The results element

A results element holds all result data collected during use of the OCIL document. This data includes not only the final results of each questionnaire, but also a breakdown of the results for each test_action and the user's response to each question. The table below lists the properties of the results element. Additional information on calculating questionnaire results is provided in Section 7.3. Note that if the results are collected during multiple sessions, that a separate set of results will be collected for each session.

results

Property	Type	Count	Description
title (element)	TextType	0-1	A descriptive heading or caption that describes the result set.

Property	Type	Count	Description
questionnaire_results (element)	QuestionnaireResultsType	0-1	A container for all questionnaire_result elements. A questionnaire_result describes the result of evaluating a questionnaire and any associated artifact_result elements.
test_action_results (element)	TestActionResultsType	0-1	A container for all test_action_result elements. A test_action_result describes the result of evaluating a test_action and any associated artifact_result elements.
question_results (element)	QuestionResultsType	0-1	A container for all question_result elements. A question_result contains the result of evaluating a question.
artifact_results (element)	ArtifactResultsType	0-1	A container for all artifact_result elements. An artifact_result contains information about the submitted artifact.
targets (element)	TargetsType	0-1	A container for all target elements. A target is a user or system from which the documented results have been taken.
start_time (attribute)	dateTime	0-1	Specifies when the evaluation of the OCIL document started, meaning when the first question was posed.
end_time (attribute)	dateTime	0-1	Specifies when the evaluation of the OCIL document completed, meaning when the last answer was recorded.

The questionnaire_results element defines the structures that contain the computed results of all the evaluated questionnaires. The properties of the questionnaire_results element are shown below.

questionnaire_results

Property	Type	Count	Description
questionnaire_result (element)	QuestionnaireResultType	1-n	Information about the result of a particular questionnaire.

The questionnaire_result element listed above has the following properties:

questionnaire_result

Property	Type	Count	Description
artifact_results (element)	ArtifactResultsType	0-1	A set of retrieved artifacts and artifact metadata.
questionnaire_ref (attribute)	QuestionnaireIDPattern	1	Identifies a particular questionnaire by its ID.
result (attribute)	ResultType	1	The result of evaluating the specified questionnaire.

16

The test_action_results element defines the structures that contain the computed results of all the evaluated test action types. The properties of the test_action_results element are shown below.

test_action_results

Property	Type	Count	Description
test_action_result (element)	TestActionResultType	1-n	Information about the result of a particular test_action evaluation.

The test_action_result element listed above has the following properties:

test_action_result

Property	Type	Count	Description
artifact_results (element)	ArtifactResultsType	0-1	A set of retrieved artifacts and artifact metadata.
test_action_ref (attribute)	TestActionRefValuePattern	1	Identifies a particular test_action by its ID.
result (attribute)	ResultType	1	The result of evaluating the specified test_action.

The question_results element defines the structures that contain the computed results of all the evaluated questions. The properties of the question_results element are shown below.

question_results

Property	Type	Count	Description
question_result (element)	QuestionResultType	1-n	Information about the result of a particular questionnaire.

The question_result element listed above has the following properties:

question_result

Property	Type	Count	Description
question_ref (attribute)	QuestionIDPattern	1	Identifies a particular question by its ID.
response (attribute)	UserResponseType	0-1	Classification of the response. If the response was a standard answer, this is set to ANSWERED. If the answer is exceptional (UNKNOWN, NOT_APPLICABLE, etc.), then this is set to the corresponding exceptional result. See Section 7.2 for a list of result types.
result (attribute)	ResultType	1	The result of evaluating the specified questionnaire.

The question_result type is extended by four other types that correspond to the four kinds of questions: boolean, choice, numeric, and string. Each of these four extensions has an answer element that contains the answer to the question. The answer's type SHALL match the type of the question. The valid mappings are shown below:

Question Type	Question Result Type
boolean_question	boolean_question_result
choice_question	choice_question_result
numeric_question	numeric_question_result
string_question	string_question_result

The artifact_results element defines the structures that contain all artifacts retrieved during evaluation and associated metadata. The properties of the artifact_results element are shown below.

artifact_results

Property	Type	Count	Description
artifact_result (element)	ArtifactResultType	1-n	Information about a particular artifact.

The artifact_result element listed above has the following properties:

artifact_result

Property	Type	Count	Description
artifact_ref (attribute)	ArtifactIDPattern	1	Unique identifier of the artifact object that describes what the artifact is about, the type of data it holds, and other metadata.
timestamp (attribute)	dateTime	1	Date and time when the artifact was collected.
artifact_value (element)	ArtifactValueType	1	Contains either the artifact data itself or a pointer to it. This is an abstract value, with child elements binary_artifact_value, reference_artifact_value, and text_artifact_value.
provider (element)	ProviderValuePattern	1	Information about the user or system that provided the artifact.
submitter (element)	UserType	1	Information about the user who submitted the artifact.

The binary_artifact_value and text_artifact_value child elements mentioned in the table above each hold both the artifact data and the Multipurpose Internet Mail Extensions (MIME) type for that data.[3]

---

[3] The official list of MIME types is available at http://www.iana.org/assignments/media-types/.

6. Content Design Requirements and Recommendations

This section defines content design requirements, including syntax and structural requirements, that an organization or product MUST follow to create and maintain a well-formed OCIL document. This section also provides recommendations for organizing OCIL content and the implications of various OCIL document design decisions. The requirements and recommendations presented in this section supplement the content data model defined in Section 5.

6.1 OCIL Document Contents

An OCIL document instance SHALL hold exactly one ocil element. The ocil element SHALL be the root XML element of an OCIL document.

6.2 The generator Element

Additional information not covered by the standard properties of the generator element MAY be supplied after those properties. However, OCIL implementations can ignore this information.

6.3 The questionnaire Element

A questionnaire acting as top-level SHOULD represent a single discrete check, such as verifying compliance with a particular recommendation or requirement. This is preferred because each top-level questionnaire returns a single result, which corresponds well to performing a single check. Also, having a single check per questionnaire provides a modular approach to questionnaire design that supports questionnaire reuse.

Each questionnaire SHALL have a unique identifier, as expressed using the id property, and SHALL be referenced through that identifier. Each questionnaire identifier SHALL use the following syntax:

```
"ocil:[A-Za-z0-9_\-\.]+:questionnaire:[1-9][0-9]*"
```

An example of this follows:

```
<questionnaire id="ocil:org.mitre:questionnaire:1">
```

Each questionnaire identifier SHOULD be globally unique. The string after `"ocil:"` SHOULD be set appropriately to accomplish this, and SHOULD specify an inverted Domain Name System (DNS) name.

Each questionnaire SHALL contain an actions element that has references to one or more test_action elements. The test_action elements within an actions element are evaluated in sequential order. Each actions element MAY also contain an operator to aggregate the test_action results and a negate attribute used to toggle the value of the final result (i.e., from PASS to FAIL, or FAIL to PASS). Although a single questionnaire SHALL NOT specify more than one operator to aggregate its test_action results, more complex aggregations MAY be performed by having one or more test_action elements refer to other questionnaires, which MAY themselves reference multiple test_action elements and aggregate them with their own operator. This allows for arbitrarily complex logical combinations of responses.

At least one questionnaire in each OCIL document SHALL have its child_only property set to false, thus allowing it to be used as a top-level questionnaire.

6.4 The test_action Element

Each question_test_action SHALL have a unique identifier, as expressed using the id property, and its child elements (boolean_question_test_action, choice_question_test_action, numeric_question_test_action, and string_question_test_action) SHALL be referenced through that identifier. The identifiers SHALL use the following syntax:

```
"ocil:[A-Za-z0-9_\-\.]+:testaction:[1-9][0-9]*"
```

Each question_test_action identifier SHOULD be globally unique. The string after `"ocil:"` SHOULD be set appropriately to accomplish this, and SHOULD specify an inverted Domain Name System (DNS) name.

Each question_test_action SHOULD be written so as to cover all of the possible answers that could be provided. If a question_test_action is not written that way, then an ERROR result will be generated if an answer is provided that the question_test_action is not designed to handle. In some cases, an author MAY choose to have a question_test_action not cover certain answers or ranges of answers so that an ERROR result is generated. Section 7.5 further discusses cases when there is no handler for an answer.

Each numeric_question_test_action SHALL be written so that its handlers are in the proper sequence if there is any overlap between the values that they handle. When looking for a match, all when_equals handlers are checked before when_range handlers, and handlers in each category are checked in sequence based on their order within the document.

Each string_question_test_action SHALL be written so that its handlers are in the proper sequence if there is any overlap between the patterns that they look for. The handlers are checked in sequence and the first one with a pattern matching the response is used.

The when_unknown, when_not_tested, when_not_applicable, and when_error properties of the question_test_action element are all of type TestActionConditionType. All of the additional properties of the boolean, choice, numeric, and string child elements of question_test_action either are of the TestActionConditionType or use a type that extends it. When determining how a test_action should handle a response to a question, the author SHALL specify either a result (a final value to be returned) or a test_action_ref (a reference to a new test_action or questionnaire to be processed), but SHALL NOT specify both.

6.5 The question Element

Each question SHALL have a unique identifier, as expressed using the id property, and its child elements (boolean_question, choice_question, numeric_question, and string_question) SHALL be referenced through that identifier. The identifiers SHALL use the following syntax:

```
"ocil:[A-Za-z0-9_\-\.]+:question:[1-9][0-9]*"
```

Each question identifier SHOULD be globally unique. The string after `"ocil:"` SHOULD be set appropriately to accomplish this, and SHOULD specify an inverted Domain Name System (DNS) name.

Each question SHALL be referenced only by question_test_action and question_result elements of the same type. For example, a boolean_question could be referenced by a boolean_question_test_action and a boolean_question_result.

The four types of child elements—boolean, choice, numeric, and string—offer different granularity for answers. The simplest is boolean, which offers two options (yes/no or true/false). The next simplest is choice, which offers a small set of options (theoretically unlimited, but each choice has to be separately enumerated, which limits the number in practice). Much more granularity is available through numbers (a wide range of positive and negative integers and decimals) and even more granularity through strings (long sequences of letters and other characters). Each question instance SHOULD use the simplest child element type that provides the necessary granularity. For example, if the author wants to get a true/false answer, the author SHOULD use a boolean_question instead of treating the answer as a "TRUE" or "FALSE" string in a string_question or having the user choose "TRUE" or "FALSE" as part of a choice_question. Another example involves numbers. Suppose that the information needed is what quadrant (0-25, 26-50, 51-75, 76-100) a quiz score fell into, and the score itself is not needed. The author SHOULD use a choice_question with four choices, one for each of the quadrants, instead of a numeric_question. A numeric_question SHOULD be used if the score itself is also needed.

Authors SHOULD use instructions elements for questions that users are likely to answer more accurately and/or easily with step-by-step instructions.

A single question MAY be referenced by multiple test_actions within an OCIL document. However, implementations presenting the question can cache the answer and reuse it instead of asking the same question more than once. If an author wants to ask a question multiple times within an evaluation because of an expectation that users might give different answers—for example, because the question is being asked within a different context—then the author SHALL define a separate question for each instance, instead of using a single question multiple times. The author SHOULD provide enough information in the question wording or in the supporting instructions so that the user can reach the appropriate answer in each instance.

6.6   The artifact Element

Each artifact element SHALL have a unique identifier, as expressed using the id property, and SHALL be referenced through that identifier. The identifiers SHALL use the following syntax:

```
"ocil:[A-Za-z0-9_\-\.]+:artifact:[1-9][0-9]*"
```

Each artifact element identifier SHOULD be globally unique. The string after `"ocil:"` SHOULD be set appropriately to accomplish this, and SHOULD specify an inverted Domain Name System (DNS) name.

There are three possible types of artifacts: binary, reference, and text. Binary and text artifacts are copied from the sources, while reference artifacts are simply references, such as URIs, to the sources. If the author has flexibility in which type of artifact to collect, particularly getting a copy of the source (binary or text) versus a pointer to it (reference), then there are some possible issues to keep in mind. References might not be global; for example, a user might provide a pointer to an internal web site that can only be accessed from the internal network. In those cases, collecting a reference artifact may be of little value. On the other hand, if a source contains sensitive information, there could be security or privacy issues with copying that information and storing the copy elsewhere. OCIL does not provide any mechanisms for protecting information. Also, if files are large, additional storage space may be needed to hold them.

The artifact element's persistent attribute and the artifact_ref element's required attribute are similar, but subtly different. Setting the persistent attribute to TRUE indicates that the artifact is time-sensitive and that if the artifact is requested, it is mandatory to provide it. Setting the required attribute of the

21

artifact_ref to TRUE indicates that for the particular artifact reference being called by a test_action, it is mandatory to provide the artifact. The same artifact could be requested in a non-mandatory manner by a different artifact_ref and test_action. If the author uses the persistent and/or required attributes to make it mandatory to supply an artifact, and the artifact cannot be supplied when evaluating the questionnaire, then the questionnaire cannot be fully completed. Therefore, authors SHOULD only make artifacts mandatory if they are truly necessary.

6.7   The variable Element

Each variable SHALL have a unique identifier, as expressed using the id property, and its child elements (constant_variable, local_variable, and external_variable) SHALL be referenced through that identifier. The identifiers SHALL use the following syntax:

```
"ocil:[A-Za-z0-9_\-\.]+:variable:[1-9][0-9]*"
```

Each variable identifier SHOULD be globally unique. The string after `"ocil:"` SHOULD be set appropriately to accomplish this, and SHOULD specify an inverted Domain Name System (DNS) name.

6.8   Circular References

There are multiple ways that circular references—elements referring to themselves directly or indirectly—can occur in OCIL documents. For example, a questionnaire or test action could call itself, or a question could have a variable that gets its value from the same question. Authors SHOULD avoid using circular references because they can prevent a questionnaire evaluation from being completed and can cause operational problems due to excess resource consumption, such as infinite loops.

7. Processing Requirements

This section describes the processing requirements that an OCIL implementation MUST follow to correctly process an OCIL document.

7.1 Questionnaire Display and Evaluation

A top-level questionnaire has its child_only attribute set to false (the default setting). A top-level questionnaire MAY be posed to a user directly or called by another questionnaire.

A low-level questionnaire has its child_only attribute set to true. This type of questionnaire is designed to be part of another questionnaire. A low-level questionnaire SHALL be processed and its questions evaluated only if called by another questionnaire; it SHALL NOT be evaluated independently.

An OCIL implementation MAY choose to display a list of all the top-level questionnaires in an OCIL document to a user, and allow the user to work through the list. An OCIL implementation SHALL NOT display a low-level questionnaire in a list of top-level questionnaires since it represents a sub-section of other questionnaires.

For each choice_question displayed to the user, the choice and choice_group_ref elements SHALL BE presented to the user in the order in which they appear in the OCIL document.

If a questionnaire evaluation is split among multiple sessions, a separate set of results SHALL be collected for each session. The start_time and end_time elements SHALL reflect the start and end time of each session.

7.2 Test Action and Questionnaire Result Types

After processing (which includes receiving the necessary responses), a test action SHALL evaluate to one result type. A questionnaire SHALL also evaluate to one result type after processing. The result value of a test action or questionnaire SHALL be one of the following:
1. **PASS.** The state or condition being tested is achieved or satisfied.
2. **FAIL.** The state or condition being tested is not achieved or satisfied.
3. **UNKNOWN.** The state or condition being tested could not be determined.
4. **ERROR.** The answer to a question was an unacceptable or unhandled value; OR an unhandled situation or system error was encountered.
5. **NOT_APPLICABLE.** The test action or questionnaire does not apply to the goal as determined by response(s).
6. **NOT_TESTED.** The test action or questionnaire has not been evaluated for the following reasons: (a) the user marked a question referenced by a test action as not tested, or (b) the questionnaire or question referenced by a test action has not been evaluated yet.

7.3 Questionnaire Result Calculation

A test action defines what needs to be tested (e.g., a question), and what action to take based on the response. An action can either be an event that triggers the next test action to be evaluated or it can simply produce a result. If the action is to produce a result, then the result SHALL be propagated up to its calling test action.

A questionnaire may contain multiple references to other test actions. To evaluate a questionnaire, each referenced test action SHALL be evaluated. The test_action elements within each actions element SHALL be evaluated in sequential order. The results of the referenced test actions are combined to produce the final result of the questionnaire. The following steps describe how the results SHALL be combined (in order):

1. The value of the operation attribute in the actions element is applied. This attribute can either have an AND or OR value. By default, its value is set to AND. The truth table below (see Table 1) defines how to combine results. A "+" sign in the table denotes the specified value and any larger value. So, for example, "1+" means any value of 1 or greater.

2. The value of the negate attribute in the actions element is applied. This attribute can either have a true or false value. By default, its value is set to false. When set to true, the result returned by the questionnaire is changed in the following way: FAIL becomes PASS, PASS becomes FAIL, and all other results are unchanged.

Table 1. Truth Table for Combining Test Action Individual Results

| Operator | Number of Individual Results | | | | | | Final Result |
	PASS	FAIL	ERROR	UNKNOWN	NOT TESTED	NOT APPLICABLE	
AND	1+	0	0	0	0	0+	PASS
	0+	1+	0+	0+	0+	0+	FAIL
	0+	0	1+	0+	0+	0+	ERROR
	0+	0	0	1+	0+	0+	UNKNOWN
	0+	0	0	0	1+	0+	NOT TESTED
	0	0	0	0	0	1+	NOT APPLICABLE
	0	0	0	0	0	0	NOT TESTED
OR	1+	0+	0+	0+	0+	0+	PASS
	0	1+	0	0	0	0+	FAIL
	0	0+	1+	0+	0+	0+	ERROR
	0	0+	0	1+	0+	0+	UNKNOWN
	0	0+	0	0	1+	0+	NOT TESTED
	0	0	0	0	0	1+	NOT APPLICABLE
	0	0	0	0	0	0	NOT TESTED

The truth table contains two entries under each operator that generate a final result of NOT TESTED. In each case, the first entry corresponds to instances where there are no individual FAIL, ERROR, or UNKNOWN results, and at least one individual NOT TESTED result. The second entry corresponds to no individual results being returned at all.

Within the scope of each operator (AND and OR), the rows in the truth table are mutually exclusive; it is not possible to have a combination of test action individual results that maps to multiple rows. Any combination of test action results will produce a deterministic final result using this table.

7.4   Test_Action Processing

Every test_action that references a question MAY contain any or all of the following elements: when_error, when_unknown, when_not_tested, and when_not_applicable. When a test_action evaluates to a value with no defined action, the result SHALL be an ERROR. For example, if a user marks a test as NOT_APPLICABLE, but there is no when_not_applicable handler, the test_action SHALL evaluate to ERROR. Likewise, if a normal answer (boolean, number, string, etc.) is provided but there is no handler for that answer, this SHALL also evaluate to ERROR. For example, if the response is 9, but there is no when_equals or when_range handlers that match a value of 9, then an ERROR SHALL be returned. This means that, apart from an ERROR result, the only time any other result values are returned by a test action would be if the handler explicitly provided a return value.

Consider the following example:

(Source: ISO IEC 27002 2005 Information Security Audit Tool)
```
8.1 Question 1.  Have you reduced the risk of theft, fraud, or misuse of
facilities by making sure that all prospective employees understand their
responsibilities before you hire them?        YES    NO    N/A
```

The question requires an answer of YES, NO, or N/A (Not Applicable). It is best modeled with a boolean_question element. For instance,

```
<boolean_question id="ocil:org.mitre:question:1" model="MODEL_YES_NO">
   <question_text>
      Have you reduced the risk of theft, fraud, or misuse of facilities by
      making sure that all prospective employees understand their
      responsibilities before you hire them?
   </question_text>
</boolean_question>
```

To describe what happens when a user responds to this type of question, a boolean_question_test_action can be defined in the following manner:

```
<boolean_question_test_action id="ocil:org.mitre:testaction:1"
   question_ref="ocil:org.mitre:question:1">
   <when_true>
      <result>PASS</result>
   </when_true>
   <when_false>
      <test_action_ref>ocil:org.mitre:testaction:2</test_action_ref>
   </when_false>
   <when_not_applicable>
      <test_action_ref>ocil:org.mitre:testaction:3</test_action_ref>
   </when_not_applicable>
</boolean_question_test_action>
```

An OCIL implementation SHALL present the referenced question. Based on the response to the question, the test action would perform different actions. Specifically, if the response is:

YES   The when_true handler is invoked, which sets the result of this test action to PASS.

NO   The when_false handler is invoked. This causes the implementation to evaluate the test action with id *ocil:org.mitre:testaction:2*. Whatever that test action evaluates to becomes the result of this test action.

| N/A | The when_not_applicable handler is invoked. This causes the implementation to evaluate the test action with id *ocil:org.mitre:testaction:3*. Whatever that test action evaluates to becomes the result of this test action. |
| Anything else | There is no handler for any other responses, so other responses set the result of this test action to ERROR. |

Note that for simplicity purposes, 'yes' and 'true' responses are mapped to a when_true element. Similarly, 'no' and 'false' responses are mapped to a when_false element.

A choice_question_test_action contains a set of when_choice elements. A when_choice element defines what action to take when the response matches one of a list of choices. The schema prevents multiple when_choice elements from containing references to the same choice within a single choice_test_action.

A numeric_question_test_action contains a set of when_equals and/or when_range elements. A when_equals element defines what action to take when a particular value matches the response. Similarly, a when_range element defines what action to take when the response is within a specified range of values, for example [29,100], [101,132), or (131, 249]. If the response matches multiple conditions, then the first matching handler SHALL be applied based on the order the handlers appear within the document. Since when_equals handlers always come before when_range handlers, preference is given to exact matches.

A string_question_test_action contains a set of when_pattern elements. A when_pattern element defines what action to taken when the response matches a particular regular expression. Similar to numeric_test_action, if the response matches multiple conditions, then the first when_pattern matched SHALL be applied based on their order within the document.

7.5 Questions with Multiple References

A single question MAY be referenced by multiple test_actions within an OCIL document. If a question has already been answered during an evaluation, the same question SHOULD NOT be answered again in the same evaluation. Instead, the implementation SHOULD cache the answer to the first instance of the question and reuse that answer when evaluating any other test actions that use the same question.

7.6 Artifact Submission

A user or system MAY be asked to submit an artifact to support a response to one or more questions within a questionnaire.

If an artifact element's persistent attribute is set to TRUE and/or an artifact_ref element's required attribute is set to TRUE, then
1. The user or system SHALL be informed that the artifact is required.
2. The artifact SHALL be collected; otherwise, an ERROR result SHALL be generated.

If an artifact element's persistent attribute is set to FALSE and an artifact_ref element's required attribute is set to FALSE, then
1. The user or system SHALL be informed that the artifact is optional.
2. The artifact SHALL be collected if the user or system supplies it; otherwise, evaluation of the OCIL document SHALL continue without the artifact collection.

7.7   Variable Processing

The value of any variable SHALL be computed before it is used.

For each local_variable, the question it references SHALL be posed before the variable's use.

The value of a local_variable is determined based on the answer to the question that it links to. The local_variable MAY have one or more set elements defined. If so, the variable's value SHALL be computed based on those set elements; the value stored in the first set element that produces a matched pattern SHALL be used. If none of the set elements have a pattern that matches the answer, then an ERROR result SHALL be generated by all referencing test_actions.

If no set element is present, the value used SHALL be the same as the answer, with a few exceptions. The value mappings are as follows:
1. If the question is a boolean question and the variable data type is NUMERIC, then the value based on the answer SHALL be 1 for true and 0 for false.
2. If the question is a boolean question and the variable data type is TEXT, then the value SHALL be determined by the question's model as follows:
    a. MODEL_YES_NO: the value is yes if true or no if false.
    b. MODEL_TRUE_FALSE: the value is true if true or false if false.
3. If the question is a choice question, the variable data type SHALL be TEXT and the value SHALL be set to the text value of the choice.
4. If the question is a numeric question, the variable data type SHALL be NUMERIC and the value SHALL be set to the value of the answer.
5. If the question is a string question, the variable data type SHALL be TEXT and the value SHALL be set to the value of the answer.

If a local variable is referenced and the value cannot be determined, then the referencing question or test action SHALL cause an ERROR result to be generated by all referencing test actions.

If the value for an external_variable cannot be retrieved from an external source, then the referencing question or test_action SHALL cause an ERROR result to be generated whenever a test_action attempts to use the variable during evaluation. If the variable is not referenced during an evaluation—for example, the variable is used by a test_action that is not called during a particular evaluation—then an ERROR result SHOULD NOT be generated.

7.8   Graceful Error Handling

When initially processing an OCIL document, an OCIL implementation SHOULD check for all forms of circular references, such as a questionnaire or test action that calls itself, and a question that has a variable that gets its value from the same question. The implementation SHOULD handle these circular references gracefully, such as producing an informative error message detailing the circular references instead of displaying questionnaires containing circular references.

An OCIL implementation SHOULD NOT suddenly terminate its execution due to an error condition. OCIL implementations SHOULD handle all exceptional conditions gracefully by performing proper error and exception handling. For all such conditions that do not have handling requirements defined elsewhere in this specification, the implementation SHOULD produce an informative error message. For exceptional conditions involving questionnaire evaluation, implementations MAY set results appropriately, based on the nature of the exceptional condition, and skip a section of a questionnaire or an entire questionnaire to allow evaluation of other questionnaires or questionnaire sections to proceed.

7.9 The generator Element

Additional information not covered by the standard properties of the generator element may be supplied after those properties. However, OCIL implementations MAY choose to ignore this information.

Appendix A—Use Cases

As discussed in Section 1, OCIL can be used in many ways to gather information from previous data collection efforts and from people. This appendix describes several common use cases for OCIL. Other use cases are possible, and the authors encourage people with additional use cases to submit them for inclusion in the final version of this specification.

Aggregating Results

OCIL can be used to aggregate results from multiple data sources.

An example is using OCIL to convert disparate information into a single standardized format. If an organization has several existing sources of system configuration management information, each of which has information on the status of configurations for various systems, applications, and other IT components, OCIL could be used to harvest information from these sources and store it in a standardized format. This aggregated information could then be combined with other sources, such as the results of OVAL evaluations, and fed into a single entity, such as a dashboard. This would allow many sources of information to be viewed and analyzed from a single interface.

Supplementing Automated System Checks

When evaluating a system, OCIL can be used to perform manual checks that cannot be performed in a fully automated manner.

An example of this is using OCIL with XCCDF. Suppose that someone writes an XCCDF document containing system security checks to collect evidence to demonstrate PCI-DSS compliance. One of the checks requires a complex evaluation that currently cannot be automated using operating system or application supported application programming interfaces (APIs). Within the document, the author includes a reference to an OCIL document containing a manual check. A security professional assigned to the task of checking the system for compliance loads the XCCDF document into an XCCDF interpreter. Upon reaching a manual check, the XCCDF interpreter loads the OCIL document into the OCIL interpreter (either through a built-in functionality within the XCCDF interpreter or an external OCIL implementation), which asks the security officer a series of questions. The security officer's responses are collected and interpreted. The OCIL results are returned to the XCCDF interpreter, which then continues with the remaining checks and generates OVAL results. The OCIL and OVAL results are aggregated into a single report by the XCCDF interpreter, which can then be used to demonstrate PCI-DSS compliance.

Collecting Information from People

OCIL can be used to collect information from people, such as their knowledge, responsibilities, interests, and opinions.

An example of this is collecting information from building evacuation coordinators, who are responsible for ensuring that employees and visitors are safely evacuated from the building during emergencies or drills. After each evacuation, all of the coordinators are emailed a request to submit an evacuation report. The email contains a link to a form on the organization's internal web site; this form is the front-end to an OCIL document. The user answers the questions in the form, such as how long it took to evacuate everyone. In some cases, the answer to a question causes different questions to be asked; for example, responding "yes" to "Were there problems during the evacuation?" would cause additional questions regarding the nature of the problems to be displayed. When the user finishes the form, the results are submitted to a repository, so that the organization's safety officials can analyze and review all the results.

Another example of this use case is collecting information during the initial planning of a system audit. Planning may involve identifying systems, networks, applications, and other IT components to be included in the audit. OCIL can be used by auditors to collect information from key personnel about these components. Since this information is collected and stored using standardized, automated means, it can be quickly evaluated by auditors, who select the components to be audited and feed the pertinent information into tools such as vulnerability assessment scanners, thus helping to automate and expedite the assessment process.

Walking Users through Instructions

OCIL can present users with instructions, as a series of steps, and ask questions along with these instructions.

An example is collecting information as part of a property inventory audit. Through an OCIL document, users are presented with instructions to guide them in determining how to identify individual pieces of property and where to find the property label. Identifying the property number may be difficult for users, so instructions may help them—for example, guiding them to the location of the label and helping them to distinguish the property number from other pieces of information on the label. Finally, the OCIL document reports the property information to a centralized repository of property asset data.

Collecting Text, Files, and Resource References

OCIL can collect blocks of text, copies of files, and references to resources (including URLs) from systems.

An example is collecting copies of a configuration file from systems. The exact file that needs to be collected from each system depends on certain characteristics of each system's configuration. This system configuration information was recently collected for a different purpose and is stored in a database. The pertinent information in this database could be harvested through automated techniques and used by an OCIL document to determine which configuration file needs to be collected from each system. The OCIL document would then transfer a copy of the appropriate file to a central server for subsequent review, along with a copy of the pertinent system configuration characteristics.

Appendix B—Use of OCIL as an XCCDF Check System

This appendix defines requirements for using OCIL as a check system for XCCDF. These requirements supplement the other OCIL requirements in this publication, as well as XCCDF requirements as documented in NIST IR 7275 Revision 3, *Specification for the Extensible Configuration Checklist Description Format (XCCDF)*,[4] and any subsequent releases of the XCCDF version 1.x specification.

B.1   OCIL <xccdf:check> Usage

References from XCCDF to OCIL questionnaires SHALL use the form:

```
<check-content-ref href="OCIL_Source_URI" name="OCIL_Questionnaire_Id" />
```

The @href attribute SHALL identify the location of the OCIL questionnaire. The @name attribute SHALL refer to a specific questionnaire identifier within the @href source. When an XCCDF rule references a specific OCIL questionnaire, an OCIL questionnaire source SHALL be available to resolve the reference.

In the syntax shown above, the <xccdf:check-content-ref> element's @href attribute refers to an OCIL questionnaire containing one or more test actions. This @check-content-ref is equivalent to *referencing* an OCIL questionnaire of the form:

```
<questionnaire id="identifier of questionnaire" child_only="false">
    <title>…</title>
    <description>…</description>
    <references>…</references>
    <actions>
        <test_action_ref>identifier of test action</test_action_ref>
    </actions>
</questionnaire>
```

B.2   <xccdf:Value> and OCIL Variable Dependencies

OCIL provides support for defining values that can be reused in stating questions and evaluating questionnaires. These values MAY be passed from XCCDF as value parameters and into OCIL as external variables.

When an XCCDF rule refers to an OCIL questionnaire requiring one or more external variables, the XCCDF rule SHALL include <xccdf:check-export> elements that define the mapping from an XCCDF value to an OCIL external variable. The format of these elements is:

```
<check-export xmlns="http://checklists.nist.gov/xccdf/1.1"
        value-id="XCCDF_Value_id" export-name="OCIL_External_Variable_id" />
```

The following example demonstrates the use of this convention:

---

[4]   http://csrc.nist.gov/publications/PubsNISTIRs.html

```
<check system="http://www.mitre.org/ocil/2">
      <check-export value-id="OnlyLaptops_var"
      export-name="ocil:gov.nist.abc.xp:var:11000" />
      <check-export value-id="HighAlertPolicy_var"
      export-name="ocil:gov.nist.abc.xp:var:11001" />
      <check-content-ref href="abc-all-ocil.xml"
      name="ocil:gov.nist.abc.xp:def:11001" />
</check>
```

The type and value binding of the specified XCCDF value SHALL be constrained to match the indicated OCIL variable data type. Table 2 summarizes the constraints regarding data type usage.

Table 2. XCCDF-OCIL Data Export Matching Constraints

OCIL Variable Data Type	Matching XCCDF Data Type
TEXT	string; boolean
NUMERIC	number

B.3   Mapping OCIL Results to XCCDF Results

OCIL supports full status reporting. See Table 3 for mapping from OCIL questionnaire results to XCCDF results. When evaluated, an OCIL document MAY contain an `<ocil:results>` element that contains all the questionnaire results, including user responses and artifacts.

Table 3. Deriving XCCDF Rule Results from OCIL Questionnaire Results

OCIL Questionnaire Result	XCCDF Rule Result
ERROR	error
UNKNOWN	unknown
NOT_APPLICABLE	notapplicable
NOT_TESTED	notchecked
PASS	pass
FAIL	fail

Appendix C—Change Log

2.0 DRAFT 1 – 24 August 2009

- Initial draft specification released to the OCIL community for comment.

2.0 DRAFT 2 – 22 October 2010 (first CSRC Draft)

- Editorial changes throughout the document. Condensed or removed most background information.
- Removed the OCIL schema appendix (Appendix A) and the OCIL content example appendix (Appendix B) from the document, and posted them online.
- Created new sections on conformance (Section 3) and OCIL's relationships to existing specifications and standards (Section 4). Created new appendix on requirements for using OCIL as an XCCDF check system (Appendix B).
- Moved the Vision for Use (Section 1.2) material into a new appendix (Appendix A), converted it into use cases, and expanded it.
- Expanded the Data Model section to include additional elements and attributes.
- Separated requirements into two sections, one on OCIL content (Section 6) and one on OCIL processing (Section 7). Moved requirements from the data model section to these sections.
- Removed the priority and scope attributes, and the PriorityType and ScopeType types.
- Made several changes to how artifact-related information is structured.
- Added the QuestionTextType type to allow substitution of local variables into question text.
- Altered how set elements are used for local variables.
- Deleted the default_value element for external variables.

2.0 FINAL – 7 April 2011

- Minor editorial changes throughout the document.
- Added discussion of applying digital signatures to OCIL results.
- Added the additional_data element to the generator element.
- Expanded the binary_artifact_value and text_artifact_value child elements to include the MIME type for the data they hold.
- Clarified the composition of the unique identifiers for questionnaire, test_action, question, artifact, and variable elements.

www.ingramcontent.com/pod-product-compliance
Lightning Source LLC
Chambersburg PA
CBHW060512060326
40689CB00020B/4713